One Petal at a Time

Joni Karen Caggiano

Published by Prolific Pulse Press LLC
Raleigh, North Carolina USA
April 2024

Contact: admin@prolificpulse.com

Library of Congress Control Number: 2024905379

ISBN 978-1-962374-16-3 Paperback
ISBN 978-1-962374-17-0 eBook

Cover and Interior Art by Francisco Bravo Cabrera
Also Known as Bodo Vespaciano

Dedication

To all children from dysfunctional families.

To the inner child who has absorbed the memories, sometimes not yet realized.

To the inner child who has come to realize that the pain of their childhood was not normal.

To the still suffering adults who desire change.

To the unspoken, the unknown who deserve to have a better life.

You are not alone.

Primrose in Winter

group of turtles without a shell

we masquerade in shadows, but all can tell

no matter what we do, as scapegoats, we exist to fail

take care of parents at age six

jumbled, frightened, a defective mix

worn away and far-flung, we ARE the angry bricks

one day a visitor, contentment, arrives

blood-stained tales, yet a warrior survives

like a lone primrose in winter who somehow thrives

Acknowledgements

Thank you to the following publications for featuring my poetry:

"Tribute to the Forest"
> *Vita Brevis*, Curator Brian Geiger, June 2020

"Melding Into You"
> *SpillWords Press* NYC – April 2021

"Lost Love"
> The *Sound of Brilliance: The Short of It, Vol. 1*
> Published by Susi Bocks, April 2021

"Memories Buried In A Box"
> *MasticadoresUSA,* Curator Gabriela Marie Milton,
> May 2021

"The Colors of Love"
> *MasticadoresUSA,* Curator Gabriela Marie Milton,
> June 2021

"You Were The Best of Us"
> Honorable Mention for Contest:
> *Woman: Splendor and Sorrow: | Love Poems
> and Poetic Prose* , November. 2021

"Lonely Employment"
>*Edge of Humanity Magazine*, Curator Joelcy Kay,
>February 2022

"Sunflower – A New Page"
>*MasticadoresUSA*, Curator Gabriela Marie Milton,
>May 2022

"Woods and Beasts," "A Tale of Two"
>*Wounds I Healed Poetry of Strong Women,*
>Published by Experiments in Fiction, June 2022

"End of The Season"
>*SpillWords Press* NYC, August 2022

"Love Me Like a Luna"
>*SpillWords Press* NYC – November 2022

"Lady of Strength"
>*MasticadoresIndia*, Curated by Terveen Gill,
>December 2022

"Cleansing," "God's Grace,"
>*Hidden In Childhood – A Poetry Anthology,*
>Published by Literary Revelations, January 2023

"Southern Rising"
>*MasticadoresUSA,* Curator Barbara Leonhard,
>January 2023

"Reflection"

> *MasticadoresUSA*, Curator Barbara Leonhard,
> February 2023

"Us"

> *MasticadoresIndia,* Curator Terveen Gill, February
> 2023

"Sadness Moans," "Uncle's House,"

> *Reflections & Revelations -The Short of It,*
> *Volume 2*
> Published by Susi Bocks, April 2023

"Full of Treasures"

> *MasticadoresIndia,* Curator Terveen Gill, April
> 2023

Table of Contents

Author's Note

A young woman shifts amid the commonalities like a chameleon. Transforming into bright sapphire colors, long and willowy movements to maintain her survival, she imparts skills perfected long ago. Crowds unnerve her, yet she compels herself to remain and make fleeting chatter. Clown-like behavior emerges as her skin crawls as memoirs written in braille, hidden beneath her pores, spit their way out. Old anxieties escalate, and she must remove the blinding red behind her eyes. Hastily she becomes the center of attention as her breath softens. Learning that her humor distracts the unpleasantness that can pierce stone or brick far beneath the surface. Vigilance is required; without it, the ceiling will collapse, and the shadow of death, plays solitaire with black keys.

Fear, an unwelcome bedfellow, slithers beside her at age five, making peaceful slumber impossible. Exhaustion during school years, and trepidation for dangers lurking at home, during her absence, would produce taxing circumstances hindering her ability to learn.

She was extraordinarily perceptive and had an astounding sixth sense. Her mind was either black or white, for the in-between did not exist. As a child, there was nothing more than either-or. If she stepped outside that boundary, threats would become a reality.

Low self-esteem grew like weeds in an unkempt garden. The desire to compete with every woman in a room became the norm. Any stranger her loved one stared at extensively brought out the lioness in her. She would don brass armor to shine like an army of soldiers or wear a skimpy dress that grasped her slight curves firmly, like bark from an iron oak. Exhaustion was the enemy as there were not enough hours to make her lists (of what she must do) to make her life calculable. Her needs were unimportant. The only thing that mattered was that everyone approved of her and that the boat never got lost at sea. She must always steer the ship to perfection. The problem, was she wasn't a sailor and she knew she needed a lifeline!

Foreword

Michelle Ayon Navajas

Joni is among the sweetest and most beautiful humans I've met on the World Wide Web. Let me start by saying she will support you with your work and the causes you believe in helping to play a significant role in our world. We bonded and shared one common goal: to help victims of abuse and violence through our written works.

I found her works skillfully, brilliantly written, and filled with "raw" and "unembellished" emotions, coming from the deepest recesses of her heart and soul, thus making them more impactful and engaging. Joni's poems and stories, whether fictional or based on her experiences, always made me cry. The opening verses of her poetry are what has always stirred me the most. She can usher you and walk you hand in hand until you finish reading and then gives you a complete halt with her epic endings, while simultaneously leaving the reader wanting more. That is the beauty of Joni's poetry. Every syllable, word, line, and verse are curated and arranged to give you the most captivating feeling as a reader. Joni masters this without forgetting that she writes for a specific reason: to create awareness. Her poems on abuse and violence are the ones that will always bring me to tears. The woman in me is aching for the pain in each of her words and crying for the injustices she faced. She also writes poetry about her childhood. Growing up with two alcoholic parents is a savage hell on earth. A child needs a safe environment with loving and nurturing parents. But what happens if that supposed environment and parents required are the same factors missing? That happened to Joni. I salute her and give her my utmost respect for becoming the strong, confident, and triumphant woman she is today. Despite all that happened to Joni, most importantly, I salute her for breaking the cycle and giving her husband and daughter a fulfilling life as a mother and wife.

Her stories are undeniably brilliant. She is a gifted and skillful storyteller. She can weave heart-wrenching "story episodes" while considering her personal experiences. She creates very graphic imagery.

When Joni shared the news of her upcoming book, I was thrilled and excited for her and the rest of the world. This book of prose and poetry will give us access to what it was like to live in her crazy home as a child and teenager. Despite her challenges, she secured a spot for all of us to see hope and light amidst the trials and tribulations she faced. In "Section Three," Joni describes how it was to survive, heal, and live as a healthy, happily functioning woman.

This book will give us a roller coaster of emotions, and as we take on the tightest grip, we experience what Joni experienced; the unbearable pain of a lost childhood, the horrific brokenness of an abused teenager, and the sigh of relief at the end.

I'd end by saying political persecution, extreme poverty, global warming, war, or hunger, may not be the most extraordinary human problem our world is facing nowadays; it is the ability to birth life to an innocent child and not being able to provide a safe and peaceful environment.
May we all learn to become responsible parents and compassionate human beings.

And to Joni, I salute you for sharing your life through your beautiful prose and poetry.

Michelle Ayon Navajas (born June 23, 1976) is a Filipino poet/writer. She is a Best-Selling international Poet known for her books reaching the #1 spot within days of their release. Her 8th poetry book, *I Am in Itself Poetry in The Dark*, went straight to the top of both the best-sellers list and new releases on Amazon on short notice. Her 7th poetry book, *It Ain't Winning If Without You*, went straight to the best-sellers list on Amazon in less than 24 hours of release by pre-orders alone and became the number poetry book on all Amazon markets worldwide on its actual release day.

Michelle holds the title of having 4 books published in a row to have made it to Amazon's Best-Sellers List, *I Will Love You Forever, Too; After Rain Skies, 2nd Edition; It Ain't Winning If Without You,* and *I Am In Itself Poetry In The Dark.* Her poetry appeared in several international literary magazines such as *Spillwords* (with two poems voted as Publication of the Month), *Masticadores U.S.A,* and India. She is *Spillwords* Author of the Month, March 2023.

One Petal at a Time

Part One

The Beginning

Blind for a fleeting measure, like the wounding experience of a bird who impetuously sees a glimpse of a tempting replication. As I soar forward, trying to fit in and hitting the glass, I am alone while desperately seeking solace. Acrid, like a bite of lemon furrowing my face, is the reality of my youth. Memories I hold knotted in a sack spun with the blood of tiny fingers. Within are monsters, wounds, and violations incarcerated. Power grows into a dam bellowing inside the fractures of my brain in prayerful aspirations for its liberation behind dark eyes.

Submerging myself, I'm in a lost body of water, and the unspeakable trepidations clawing at me for fortification do not appear to exist. The undefinable realities of that brief period we know as childhood lie concealed and dormant amongst the bricks. Fear builds itself by closing the holes of light that stroll in the darkness. What I don't see can't truly hurt me, or can it? I am the watcher of monsters slumbering with lit cigarettes, abandoning hot iron, stove, and oven. Emotionally exhausting, my allegiance is, with great care, to keep the two imitators unscathed. My fledgling face holds a lingering crimson path, where tears fall incessantly carving my saga.

Creeping eyes make their secret inspections before it is safe to leave the house. Blood-shot, six-year-old eyes progress twenty times over each burner, across cords leading to outlets, and checking ashtrays. I must purge myself of visions of flames leaping hastily, like a grasshopper away from the end of my fishing hook. Weariness and hunger pains set in before school.

A female intruder divulges her terrifying stories about her dead sister's visit. Chills trigger goosebumps that, as predicted, stand to attention! Does evil lurk within the hollows of the breaths I grasp for good measure? The foretelling of someone drowning or snakes warrants some unknown family member's curtain will indeed close. Death seems a frequent visitor that hovers over this house. Only two days after Mom's vivid proclamation of death, she again proclaims her accuracy. A drunk uncle drowns in his pond, and his wife finds him floating by his miniature wood boat alongside his fishing pole. The Red Brick House is frightening with monsters and notes of the dead who skulk. Like an embracing vine covering my tiny body, I am the voice of fear enclosed in nature's dress.

As mosquitoes rise in summer, so mysteriously does an unknown family. God spreads out a bouquet of nature, and I hide within offerings of swimming, fishing, and an auntie with skin allergic to God's sun. Like vipers striking at innocence, two uncles emanate in the guise of delicate weavings of music, dancing, and sleepovers. Vibrating non-existing hips, following my uncle's orders, I sit in a soft lap that instantly transforms into hardwood. Thick tongue diving down my tiny throat, his skin folding like a rough napkin. ATTENTION – SOMEONE LOVES ME! Secrets like hairy figs grow rotten. They spread mold spores, and people find out as words carry and stick to walls with ears.

Trees brought beetles and birds to meet me on the big four. They adopt me, and I cook for fairies and angels. Sand patties mix with mud, baking in the hot, humid North Carolina sun as we sing with nature. Within the forest, peace finds me like a lost sparrow, and time no longer ticks moments of sorrow. Imagination takes me within her white wings and flies me to places only my mind can fashion.

Bitter persimmon voices yell their spiny threats my way as darkness sets horrors in play as the red bricks begin to tumble. Smiles, make-believe faces, for I am the great pretender. I must endure and survive my captivity. Tears flood my scarlet land for years until the great sun dries my sorrows.

Seed

within a minuscule drop of rain
an upside-down magnolia leaf
cradles a cone of dazzling red seed
in fall, dropping from the safety
of a stunning deep-rooted tree
thick spiny pod opening door
born an unpropitious seed, like me
floating, nine months in the salty sea
creating another aspiring branch
upon my curious family tree

Noisy Thoughts in the Night

engulfing the ominous shadows
haunted by fearful noises, circling
in the red brick house as it battles

frightened, I hide my innocent face
evil leaching off of crimson concrete
under cold sheets, beetles alter pace

darkness, dots of black and white
wild face, craziness, will she come
blackness like fog tugging on fright

crawling, tender body parts I shield
primal map of my red cement floor
children not in a position to yield

forever, I beg her to stop, please
yet I shall die on that red cement
mind drifts to sun and clapping trees

in the woods, I will find a new friend
tomorrow while I play with my doll
magnificent the forest, its voice the wind

hoping for my freedom and an early spring
asking the Lord, I bow my head to pray
tell me, what echo of night owls might bring

Cleansing

silence is the tiptoe
of a fairy as she slyly
births comfort
youthful dreamer
writing love notes to pixies
in beams the moon can spare
solace wrapped
in prayer under covers
phantom of shame circles
disgrace like fireflies
without flames
ladybugs missing spots
and archaic tainted statues
with long-ago muted tongues
while willows lament
so, plug your ears
if puffed up, with moss
from primal oaks if truth offends
boulders of disgrace grow roots
in cotton pockets as relics
intuition dots vistas
piercing words of neighbors
school faces bestowing nicknames
drilling holes in fragility
vultures with verdicts dripping
from shallow humans
point at me in devil's regalia
no more uncle's probing privates
entwining among protective
bark of hollow trees

hope nurtures a spirit of wind kisses
falling gently on unsure budding face
nights bring gifts of petrichor
sleep grooms my body
God's cleansing rain

Southern Rising

snow lays reticent, a virgin blanket
covers nature like a gentle quilt
thick white breath journeys on
through dated chimney stones
black iron stove warms mama
making flour bread in iron skillet
tiny portions of salt pork, browns
smell of fresh coffee clings to walls
grits gurgle in pot, red-eye gravy
sizzles in sauté pan, a southern relish
sun shines on icicle, prism of crystal
stirring as music notes shift in song
blue jay mimics hawk, on winter holly
aromas dance in air like magic
dough rising in twin wood bowls
along with smiles of my expectation
beams of love given through a meal
dusting small hands on flour sack apron
cinnamon buns like bites of heaven
rise, buttered, and served by seven

Lonely Employment

you ride your bike, crying down the hard dirt road
your morning spent killing flies
their price, a penny a carcass
handing you money through the soul of a drunken hollow
you wonder, would they spend a penny for you
buying fire balls in a brown paper bag with pennies
they torture the tongue, geographical as it was
it seems you are a rarity for the military doctors
you stick paintbrush handles up your nose
and bubble gum when its sugar is gone
anemic, they threaten you with blood transfusions
sounds interesting to you, riding home with your goodies
now you kill flies on the outside of the door
of red brick house, your bedroom with its cold red floor
you collect copper-colored prizes
but not for a while, soon they will be sick
lonely employment for the sober

Reflection - Prose

White is the oval mirror of my exodus from the fearsome actions of the monsters in the red-brick house. Dark eyes blister as my heart pulses a bleak opus once again. An offering given by a stranger concealed with golden paper and wildflowers singing. After five years of her pleasure, I perceive the wonder of the gift and grasp the stranger's identity. Such a beautiful thing I had never seen. Her face was an alluring light, blazing like the sun, for she was an angel.

Gazing intently into the mirror, I quickly initiate the smooth passage of her gelatinous cavity. My slip is now a glowing covering of layer upon layer of silk worthy of a queen. Greetings take place from the mermaid who visits from the pristine waters. Her voice comes forth like a rainbow of colors. Purple periwinkle smells of freshly baked cookies. Humans with incandescent wings sit on green moss that never stops humming. Sacred is the knowledge the purple birds share as they fly in this world of peaceful beings.

Green vines climb daily, covering this world with the fresh smell of love, laughter, and harmony. Elves wander close to hoary trees talking in the language of our Maker as they sit on the shelf of her noble roots. Thereupon the thickset moss is the mother of all fairies. When she speaks, even hummingbirds in torpor withdraw from hibernation to listen. In anticipation, I wait when this world of bliss suddenly begins to move in waves and a loud sound penetrates her graceful curves.

I'm now back in my room. My feet feel the cold of the red concrete floor, and my bed is still unmade. My mother is drunk, pulling my hair, as once again, I grow small. Her words pierce like a shard of glass in my heart. I pray she overlooks the small piece of white silk hanging from my oval mirror.

Drifting Thoughts

on a leaf, with an elf, I drift like a cloud
with giggling smiles back into my room
eyelids, cautious, yellow muted shutters
veiling them with bright clean sheets
dried in sunny breezes dancing a jig
silence was my burden and my ally
heaving memories, a dragging chain
caterpillar stirs in small silk cocoons
in a country far away, they work and spin
wind rustles leaves gifting exquisite seeds
fragrant honeysuckle through red bricks
my mother's hand once tenderly rubbed
my feverish forehead when I was five
a ballerina stands on tippy toes in mid-air
turning to the sound of magical time
grateful as I awaken to the fleeting song
of a blue jay's rhyme as a cricket sings along

Silent Cry

walking fast as sand grass

thrashes my skinny legs

drunken monster forgot

a bottle at the neighbors

sent to fetch in ghastly weather

rain needles my pound of flesh

begging God to take me now

My Almighty, at six I holler

I quiver, shaking small fists

in sticky air, anemic arms,

held high, must I always fear

drunken monsters who linger here

lightning cracks, a lariat bellows

God hears silent cries of innocents

I say the words, as a surprise bolt

splits hoary oak tree, I hear the roar

of the glorious hands who claw the sea

knowing God is still, here with me

A Tale of Two

into blue orbs I rest my lamenting heart now tranquil
white ravens cleanse my crestfallen and faithful soul
starlings reflect my warrior shield on cerulean skies
suffering fragile child, now limitless no longer hides

silent and rusty the barrel of dad's old pal, his shotgun
thick smoky tongues, memories of painful long fingers
slumbering in monster shadows amid timid raised brow
no doors or boundaries so what icy evils may happen
now

fear lags discarding smells of piss, rum, and vile bodies
four EMTs put her naked thrashing form on a gurney
recalling kissing cheeks of a snotty foul unshaven face
helping to clean buckets of mom's blood beating in
place

Memories

one season morphs

into another

minds reminiscing

childhood wonders

smells of gardenias

eating figs dipped

in raw sugar

hiding behind oaks

playing hide and seek

catching tadpoles

in nearby ponds

chasing fireflies

saving bubblegum

on the headboard

of my small bed

kneeling meekly

saying prayers

Prayer

in a misty, baffling space
caught snugly in between
house and age-old oaks
stood a quaint, brick abode
where odd moisture grew
searing tears deep within
mortar holding ruby bricks
woeful child noisily abides
echoes release her weeping
candid childhood prayers
seasoned with daily fears
tenderly fireflies illume
igniting a path of hope
drying her innocent tears
nature pledges joyous years

Sadness Moans

shooting pain lurches like a stranger in the blackest night
where monsters live, release their copies, swarming past,
out of sight

jealousy walks on rugged stones stealing from the gifted
holding hands of small cactus plants until the desert sands
are shifted

behind their peering eyes a Judas runs to throw a stone
whiffs of his betrayal, climbing to the top of the field,
I hear his moan

trust a blanket, with a thousand promises, tickling me
deceit, painful rubbing of an alligator's bony plates, I run to
a forest tree

a stranger in this house of horrors, yet I have to live
stealing glances, taking chances, as I taste the bitter love
I cannot give

Painful

three fine dresses
bought every year
one I wore twice
a red dress, really nice

my ballerina one
with lots of crinoline
like my fairy's dress
it made me look my best

my fairy lived in a jar
underneath my bed
feeding her sugar figs
she lay on soft hay and twigs

I wanted so badly to wear it
an extra day one week
I felt so beautiful that day
mom still had to get her way

tight around my neck
went her sweaty hands
two thick fingers got in
unable to breathe, determined to win

buttons a popping and lace
tearing and mom swearing
I left my body there for a bit
seems her yelling slowed as she hit

my favorite thing I owned
she was evil, not my mom at all
my dress lay round legs in shreds
big blue sash in tiny, battered threads

that's what you get, you see
for breaking my rules, pick it up
she threw ice cold water on my face
now only two dresses to wear every place

I hated her voice, sounds of her words
a lizard like tongue that would hiss
meanness that would grow like vines
God spoke to me often
during these times

Seven

is it true

do good children

go straight to heaven

beatings, reminders

to be good

pick your switch

weeping, searching

for skinny one

won't hurt so much

mom got her token

words unspoken

drunk, again

switch whips round

scrawny legs

welts bleed

leaves trail

one more

sad tale

March Day

lady bugs let

two twin crickets

play connect the dots

on their beauty spots

praying mantis

palms close together

on jasmine's aromatic pew

lone bee floats in magnolia's dew

moth squirms

breeze plays in wind

a parachuting joro spider's web

God nourishes, all creatures fed

Uncle's House

memories grow roots that spring up like dandelions on
a freshly mowed lawn
hiding among floating clouds, unwanted hands, or
those thin leafless limbs
the taste of cigars on lips or the slimy feel of uncle's
probing thick tongue
he took me to church, liked to watch me dance and
listen when I sang hymns

lots of summer afternoons, I sat for hours while the
birds sang songs to God
his lap was big, and it felt good to have someone to
care what I liked to do
summer days remind me of candy, fishing, and rum
bottles hiding everywhere
the smell of marigolds or that living room and wiggling
to get away from you

Waiting Still

evening the cry of the whippoorwills

open doors of love repeating their name

hundreds of times without rest

throw open the tiny wooden window

despairingly, I watch

tri-colored bat convenes with peepers on laurel oak

voices submerge my sorrows

believe time echoes her season

angels unfold their immense wings

hover close, for at a moment's notice

to take my young soul to heaven

heartstrings fasten to distant stars

fledglings part the safety of their nest

angel trumpet tired, she weeps sweet scent again

nightly prayer that I might feel and see

moonflower open at dusk to hear my plea

the face of God while holding me

Where Are You God

leaves on Japanese maple, fall like capsized tears

neglecting cones of salt, singing their lullaby

angels flutter, listening to trees chatter

bendable breezes, guarding creatures resting on moss

ivy weaves its delicate lace, as it glides

upon screen porch attaching itself like a lure

providing warmth for the chilly frogs

anticipating moths sticking to the spider's web

red rain begins to fall with vigor

encroaching while attacking the small roof

creating a relaxing, yet frightening sound

thunder begins to shout at the earth

for injustices done to those who dare not speak

of such things, I look out my small window

sheet lightning can be seen across the lands

their natural fireworks, a delay echoing

harsh sound accompanying each white flash

seen from miles around as if the devil is calling

parents stolen like day old bread

experiment gone awry, mom and dad swapped for robots

years of terror melding together

like a warm plastic puzzle

mom's time spent cooking gone

morning's breath was blood drippings

instead of bacon fat cooking

eggs and red-eye gravy

mixing with scarlet color against white porcelain

that brown drink, calling her, for breakfast

bottles play hide and seek

nurses at school, give me crackers

and coke to fill my hungry belly

saying my prayers, soothing is the rhythmic dance

of the raindrops on the roof

I ball up in a fetal position, I can feel God

yet I also feel my anger and wonder why

must you leave me here, JUST let me die

Alone

shadow of dread folds
consuming light, leaving fear
dad disappears one day
terror squeezes knotted noose
where – she would not say

mom got a job as a waitress
gives me quarters to iron her apron
starching uniform just right
black skirt, white lace for hair
afraid, now alone, she leaves me there

happy humming with delight
old southern songs as she prepares
make-up, red lipstick, box bleached hair
trees bid me goodnight, lone wren sings
choking back tears, mom does not care

Morning Promise

solace seeks translucent colors of blue jays

songs awaken small dusty heart with new color

wrens loudly proclaim the glory of a buttery sky

opening nature's window in my red brick room

marigolds hold off bugs with their foul smells

leaves saluting good morning with alert stems

lingering smell of petrichor from early shower

a good morning greeting from God my Father

Mom's Comfort

caught in a murky hole
cave wet, more like a well
when I sleep at dusk
nightmares meet me
waiting for sad eyes to shut
tossing me stiff into the hole
rocks bloating, grasping nails
ripping fingers as I fall
but I never hit the bottom
crying, I tell mama my dream
don't ever hit the floor
for you will be dead,
no longer here any more
bashing little skull on well floor

My Clever Friends

two pins and thin red thread

from mom's sewing box I snatch

dreams of joining roving circus

placing large black ants

on towering high wire

easily taught, perfectly perform

learning tricks within a day

now ice-cream sticks

planted in compact dirt

creating the wire so much higher

lady bugs, and grasshoppers

wishing I knew other kids

I would sell tickets for my show

joining the circus with such pride

my secret friends all by my side

Dinner Time

isolated and lonely

childhood echoes

no borders, no doors

bent gruesome veracity

talk, a sin not tolerated

praying not to breach

rules in place to teach

living inside a sphere

God's shelter made for me

mine consisting of the

world of vast oak trees

holding wide limbs out

greeting me every one

at dusk, the beetles

sew illumine blanket

making daylight trail

for me to follow home

where I sit at sad table

not a word was I to speak

drunken smells of ugly beaks

Tulip Shining

deep down low in the dark damp earth
even the grubs and the moles dare not go
where earthly souls of frightened wee ones
afraid of their own parents sink to hide
their tender dark-blue souls hidden inside
wrapping ourselves in vibrant imaginings
seeking to turn the dark upside down
memories that hold the sunshine inside
tulips, lone bees will pry the flower open
for pollen and a word of kindness spoken

Under the Khaki Tent

I write weaving lines of agony, a heavy crown I wear

young girl with weary eyes she must never shut

shifting white sand views moon underneath

the khaki tent, where I would stay till dusk

to stray from the fruit of discipline, Lord exempt me

hardship sunflowers do not endure

my ritual beatings not because I was bad

if I could just be better dad would not drink

swinging leather belt landing on youthful bare buttocks

rubbing my sore bottom for the longest time

survived the agony of living this boozy ballet

in that house of crazy

I spent every moment I could to fly away

in the woods till the line of

right and wrong grew hazy

The Gift

the red cement floor
creates an indoor breeze
to cool and comfort me
from the ravages of heat
sad tendrils grew long
of this unsure thing like
furry mold sticking to
heart strings which long
to be held, comforted
dad did not grasp love
one night he came home early
to bestow a gift to me
watching my dad break the
jaw of a dog he barely knew
shaking creature, unaware of
new surroundings, jumping
towards me, forbidden,
his boot hit the dog, his head flat
on the red floor, while dad
stomped and stomped
tied him up to a tree, half dead
entrenched upon my heart and soul
like me he never would be whole

in agony not much left of his head
by noon dad reporting, he will be dead
still days, his cries, live inside my head

Imagination

sleep, precious child

forget the pain

frozen, abysmal days

God's notes in rain

invisible, clown

without laughter

paints sad frown

poured out on floor

ride your magic carpet

dancing amid blue

God holds you tight

fly high little one

rejoice in glorious flight

just don't be late for dinner tonight

Something Missing

metal bugs and ivory rugs

trees that speak, doll that sings

children disappear on butterfly wings

escape safe, into my place

harm floats away on buttery bread

children sleep without peril in their bed

morning hair, sit in chair

mom pulls so hard my head will bleed

coke and crackers the nurses will kindly feed

robots drink and often stink

one day my parents will be back

love, food and caring I will no longer lack

Spreading Vines

echoes slither

snakes eat alarming facts

lies burn slow

like candle wax

linoleum breeds

scary timeworn faces

omen warns sightseers

of unwelcome places

fearful, discolored stains

youthful consummation

of circadian fear

unholy habitation

abuse spreads

like persisting vine

veiling her without a sign

growing up a slave to time

Part Two

Seedling

Warrior shields hold great strength, like the immense ironwood tree engraves arcane tears of blood that this brave youngling wears. Her full crest borne on her chest is a mystifying reminder of her youth. Like the Loggerhead Sea Turtle, my potency can endure the blows of thousands of pounds of abuse and pain without death. I turn myself inside out and gaze upon the broken insides that are me. Grasping a faucet, never turned on, like a creek, I realize I need a river of love with which to link. Opening a sunray, jovial was the Lord, hearing my prayer, delivering hope in a six-foot tall cool drink of water.

Valiant, prince of my dreams, you unbridle silken knots sustaining my fragile heart in place, like an angel sent to protect and cultivate my roots. Walking into class with a gust of transcendent rapture, I know you to be a gift from God. Your blue-green eyes could not look away from mine. Spellbinding a man of your beauty gives me strength to lean upon my fearlessness. Love felt like a wonderment, and my shield melting like chocolate in my youthful mouth in front of your gazing eyes.

Great is the gift of love wrapped in the spilling of your words upon a virgin body and soul. I fuse a bond with a tie to nature's own heart. I absorb years of splendor that even the sky could not reproduce in her morning or evening displays of colors that artists yearn to capture. Love, ultimately the intruder of all senses, grow flowers of such fragility from each pore of my being, I become a crystal garden. Even more fragile, more vulnerable was I. Only you could water my heart with one touch, one taste from your warm lips.

Slowly emerging, bequeathing a gift that no words can measure. Eyes piercing like an ocelot and hair shimmering like undulating waves of an ocean's symphonic melody.

Still, earth's jaws mangle me with her metal, leaving pieces of my brokenness roaming as spoondrift from the eastern coast. Footpaths design white sand cumulated by seagulls and little ones building castles made of unbruised and unsullied dreams.

Even love, Mom made into something foul, letting me know she inspected my panties now, when doing the laundry. A warning of such harsh sorrow, one to let me know she was watching me and my first boyfriend. Tender are we, like pure white swans entwined one into the other. Stealing images of innocence forever imbedded into my compassionate soul, for she is the snake.

Mom writes cementing in ink, "My voice is gone," on a small piece of paper, presenting it before I had my breakfast, and she was gone. Although drunk, her voice was stolen like a dying crow, choked off by some unknown and worrisome entity.

Saturday's blow dryer outside their door hid their drunken laughter and any sign of pleasure. A virgin I was, and a virgin I would stay, convinced sperm could crawl like a snake, with split tongue from any inanimate object. That sperm would wait for an unsuspecting and foolish young woman, and it would crawl up her leg into her womb, creating an unwanted soul.

Crazy was the day's word, and I was their innocent puppet. I was living for and counting the hours until I found myself enclosed in your arms, wiping my tears away and tempering my pain with your love. We were part of one another, two pieces, sewn into a quilt for life.

Love, an emotion new to me, I wrote songs in kisses and words trembling, dancing in notes that only you knew how to play.

Existence was a gift for the first time … until it wasn't.

Lockless

keyless is my lock

yet I surrender myself utterly

thinning skin with shadows

whispers and prickling flesh

secrets buried beneath a stratum

of my dried and crackling crust

haunting heart hungers

for a yielding stillness I can trust

until my essence, sweetly scented

fades timidly back to ash and dust

struggling to forget that remembrance

resemble an unmarked grave

magical innocence lost in fall's carpet

golden dry leaves free-fall, forgotten times

buried just beyond massive willow oaks

of my youth and its crimes

colors mix with nature's caress

fresh air that carries me lovingly away

disquieting nightmares

swiftly strike their sword to diminish childhood play

for now, carved a shelter delicate

yet strong, like an egg's armor, where I feel safe

my breath a song that sends forth

my overwhelming love for nature's reverent place

upon the wings of a sparrow

or the red chested bleeding-heart dove

coming safely here to cry tears of dancing joy

today I saw reflected, upon another child's face

yes, peace beckons, and lightning bugs

circle sweet gardenias in a vase

where locks don't exist, fairies sing and angels stand

and guard my magic place

Counting Clouds

sun release your hoarded heat

take-off spring's sunglasses

warm our impish youthfulness

like homemade muffins

pores germinate honeysuckle

meadow whiffs of fresh cut hay

rolling off grandma's quilt

white peasant blouse displays pale skin

caressing my shoulders with hot kisses

my mouth succumbs to unmapped

territory, I lay my head upon new tulips

once worth the same as a diamond, not to me

tallying clouds, tenderly you say the words

I love you, I always will

my brown eyes drip

honey that leaves a path

of lover's unwritten prose

past my chin's quiver

Forks of Ivy

within the choices, the ivy threads enlace through

patterned, worn, and tattered pieces of my youth

its blood a mixture of punctures that weave circles

of skin and bone into forgotten stories

tucked in corners where candy corn and ice cream drips

dried, like ink on memoirs now drawn into dust devils

along a path of smiles without corners

cigarette hanging like a tired aching pig's tail

apple pie, reaching forward to grab a knife to cut

sober days a treat left cooling in windowsill

stars sailing on the hook of the half-moon

smells traveling to the old willow oak as sap drips

absorbing the smell within her bark

longer fork, like parchment paper, tender

under hand-made buttermilk biscuits

hair falling below her hip-less figure

still developing breast, the color of cream

her bony legs tingle as jasmine mingles with long dark hair

an unbroken reminder of her prison

the seemingly endless maternal threat to prune

jasmine nightly, as slumber regrettably blows

encasement of foreboding

tiny this creature, sequestered, who knows no one

her senses ripe with emotion

hankering for the soothing southern silence

trusting only the green wisdom of wildwood creatures

that tarry, within the brief inhale, of yellow- pine dust

an acrid fork of asphalt jungle follows a creek that bleeds

tears of red dots with names of pharmaceutical drugs

meeting patients, embracing as one would

a precious soul, journey nearly ending, no one left to care

she feels their pain like an animal dying in hunter's trap

travels away from the vein of life's reality

she climbs in bed with a dying woman

with no hair who smells of death

petitions silkworms to weave canopies of comfort

praying for nature to send the bees with pollen

from fields of lavender to sprinkle their golden gift

her fork in the ivy visits all who left before her

veins slowly stop their pulsing as greens turn to browns

a trumpet moves with one bold black line, she drowns

amidst heavenly creatures a celebration of angelic sounds

sweet the smell of those waiting where the forks meet

a feast for her soul is beginning, as God calls let's eat

Woods and Beasts

even small horror bellows weary

this bedfellow I did not invite

no fairy tales or pleasure to reveal

stitch up my eyes, a dismal sight

daytime as daunting as a livid sunset

ballerina dress torn to a shred

my snot into a couch, I would smear

pulls strains of hair off my head

afraid she would leave me at a store

pores bleed, how I yearn to die

fear swells like a black prickly thorn

monsters lurk close where I lie

their diet, liquid, one calling forth beasts

fear howls, wishing I was not born

old and tired in my teens, yet wise as owls

praying I will no longer be forlorn

dancing junipers and snowy cottonwoods

call my name in a woody braille

God smiles within a brow of a bright star

this will not always be my sad tale

only those that own sight will see my scar

Lady of Strength

the glimmer of hope

hiding in the reflection

of earth's regal eyes

last petal of a floret

hangs heroic in cold wind

star visits dipped

in chocolate sings to me

lady of perpetual strength

I fly toward the sun

cirrus clouds as wings

my chariot flies to the echo

of prayers going skyward

Love Can Be Painful

adrift in soft white thoughts
outings to secret place near rainbows end
parking in your dad's new station wagon
quilts breathing fresh aromas, our special place
lily pads that sing and cattails that dance for only us

kisses touching so soft, almost lost
exploring young bodies sweetly, tenderly
your touches, my desire, my choices, never
do you push your desires onto me, my beloved
pulling long skirt above my knees, splashing in the pond

dusk creating red silk
of her lazy light in singing sky
streaks bent by oaks and pines sigh
love is both splendid and painfully brilliant
physically my body aches when we are apart my love

photographing me
seaweed, inhaling water hyacinth
plucking its purple flowers, placing them in my hair
sand grass gently waving, in timeless soft evening breezes
forever bonded to this land ... yes, forever

Forced Submission

a tortured soul,

brink of insanity

dark eyes stare

wildly, begging

extending legs

segments of a spider

fighting, a drowning fly

or a bug, kids have

picked the wings off

brain evoking burnt cats

dangling from ancient oaks

cruel kids kill innocent animals

terrifying fledgling eyes

observing mom

thrashing helplessly

using belts securing all four

bruising limbs to bedposts

red washcloth stuffed

in her gagged and muted mouth

eyes beginning to swell

sounds like a wild animal

whose flesh rips ensnared

staring, mom's eyes beg again

torment, anguish captured in shutters

of mutilating frames of a camera

which play on repeat

like a black and white

movie in my head

easier to forget this

if I pretend it is not real

shutting the door to my room

pretending a bug is stuck

in spider web, thrashes to be free

praying dad does not come

to do the same to me

Our Pond

feathers shift tickling softness

fingers dance silent ballet

shadows of silk scarf tracing

browning skin laying on blanket

summer kisses smiling cheeks

tadpoles frolic near pond's edge

dusk moves like a quiet sigh

until spring peepers sing an opus

laughter riding hope, a saving grace

looking in rear-view mirror I see

photographs of time in our place

Gifts of Winter

nature plays fiddle sweet

snow reflects sun crystals

lingering aster left by deer

blue birds give thanks to God

limbs break as if small twigs

weight of snow claims a fee

sun dims, as ardent tears

dampen fire with wonder

baritone voice of bullfrog

sings with wrens as they

drink from rain gutters

clouds alter their fluffy size

red-tail hawk makes an arrival

squirrel conducts nature's revival

Us My Love

earth churns
crying her tears
rapt in only you
inhale smells of oud
moonbeams call
stirring, I lean in
adrift without us
hunger for words
bedevil my heart
brush me faithful
moon pulls us
interwoven as a
monarch to cocoon
owls talk in riddles
becoming one
nature elongates
our feet to roots
centuries pass
broken clock
sensing God's love
time eternal
still, I dream of you
your love

was not forever

God never did

forsake me

when you left me

for another

Silence

stare at the moon, but do not claim to know her
gaze into wrinkling skin yet it holds no words like paper
no one knows my heart which hangs loosely upon
silken thread woven by a worm who truly sees me
don't dare touch me without a note or invitation
I am the black notes that play backward and can
flounder and cry devoid of permission of the wild
wax tears stain the downcast magnolia leaf all alone
last of the crickets, he slowly moves with cold limbs
red ants burrow as they feel winter's weary hand
trees rest, with their blanket of moss, their empty
spaces make room for squirrels to dart and play
sun lowers, the wren and sparrow drift off to sleep
you think I do not feel your betrayal, my winter's cold
silence slices pieces of me, an icicle, the lies you told

Blood Orange

lifeless and innocent is my fruit
bruising turns blue than brown
penetrating skin, causing sorrow
praying for a harmless tomorrow

beautiful oranges surrounding me
blood drips from internal wounds
shuddering in the shadow of dusk
dying bit by bit without any trust

tales of me drowning in the tub
nude dancing on a table of a friend
I tape my ears and fight my fears
perishing orange tree from my tears

alone my wee fruit prays to God
making doors much more secure
years pass skin now pink and red
so beautiful, no more tears to shed
my heart and fruit a thousand fed

Changes

crimson creek sighs
singing blue notes
whip-per-will neglects
his evening performance
no singing his name
holly drops her berries
moss on crepe myrtle
cries an olive tear
wincing at earthly woes
torment laments azure
angel lands softly
trees begin to clap
nature awakes as if
from a year-long nap
a wren loudly chirps
of hope and healing
thinking of God's grace
upon my heart I place my hand
and bend my knees on holy land

Sorrow

hanging by fingernails
to the air in my room
you inhale my very breath
suffocation withers me
my heartbeats hang like
old Christmas ornaments
from your skin, now searing
old flames that tell half truths
promises burrow like moles
you open your mouth, gone
an experiment was I to you
you douse our fiery red to blue
your snake like promises, die
as my hopes and prayers go by

What If

bereft of vacationing monarchs
his full lips, endlessly hot, arousing my heart
butterflies whose spots I see on sidewalks
gardenias whose smells choose not to stay
emotions I endure when you go away

coral red, blue and violet without enough algae
to be fluorescent, our rainbows under water
how my legs neglect to skip or even hop
tide forgetting to move unearthing its treasure
pressure does not rise in maples giving pancakes pleasure

bereft of vacationing monarchs
cheeks misplace hot kisses left on these lips
another feels that love and safety I once wore
when a boomerang glides heedlessly away
but unbeknown to me, finds an excuse to stray

betrayal, love for years gone without a trace
my heart stops, a gust pulls me to an abandoned place

God's Grace

love arrives like a cloud ballet

holding serenity like pearls smiling

naivety reveals me no longer faceless

for forgiveness dwells within

clear as crystals, I am not a starling

to fashion patterns for your dresses

my wings tremble not for you

yet I embed your words in memory

no longer do I need a reservoir of tears

my eyes bellow no longer

cypress trees, ponds and crawdads

sing of a lover's pale blue path

injustices touch many, my heart is not callous

God is my redemption, my salvation

resilient as mountains that slice borders

yet greet soft pigments of sunrise

owls call to the stars to bring compassion

to end suffering and pain

riding with strength of the majestic gypsy horse

smelling the scents that hover over the sand of oceans

I am at peace

Closure

expectations incarceration
tangle into a web of lies
holding a locket of his hair
wings of tiny, dried flies

lies are like venomous paste
sticking to memories light
you too, were ashamed of me
now you both linger in my night

why must your girlfriend laugh
no grace given, even for a bit
jumping into her convertible
missing your laugh, your wit

flowers no longer bloom for me
going to work after school I cry
did she have to be my friend
hoping you live to regret your lie

reaching out years later, your mom
remembers me, so kind and warm
my prayer was closure, peace for us

you died from a fall, likely already dust

in heaven we will love again this I trust

Lost Love

How your scent permeates the covers
of the bed, now wet with my doleful tears.
I visualize how we paved a path with sunlit pearls
of our feverish passion throughout the years.

Can't you hold me, my love, just once more
so I can see you in stargazed light?
Please breathe me in like only you can
just for one more delicious, and moon-kissed night.

Half a person when you are not with me,
for I am wayward in an unnerving sea of sorrow.
I cannot bear the empty wish or the wind-swept truth
of such a dispassionate tomorrow.

The denseness of my burdens without you
are oppressive and impossible to bear.
Music no longer renders its exquisite notes for me,
but you no longer profess to care.

Did I forsake the daunting waves that rule the sea,
or the love that I gave to thee?
So, for now I shall turn to liquid, for without you, love,
I no longer wish to be.

When you find the puddle of remembrances on the floor
don't be sad,
You gifted me a glimpse of what undying love is like
and what I have had.

If you return, place me on a boulder in a stargazing jar
and my floodlight will be your beacon.
My heart will shine bright, and for you, my darling,
my light will never weaken.

Lost Season

tasting you

like yesterday's

summer sky

feeling you

shiver when

we both hold

one another

to breathe goodbye

holding you

days of the lover

mourning that

sultry passion lost

my love always, it seems

comes with a painful cost

Hollow Death

tears tell stories
within a bubble
grows torment
my leaking heart
what did I do
how could he
the stars made love
while he caressed
my neck with his
mouth, but was it
me, who he thought of
ten years he lied
my body grieves
tenderness drips
like a tree's maple
barren, a frozen
death, you did this
now I must pray
but I am angry, even
at you God, these
were my days of
contentment but
they were built on

lies while clawing

tore my dress and

sip my sorrow from

a bowl of regret

perfume with no scent

time without minutes

you without me and

I without you, for

I am the death of

pale moonflower

its loss of love and

the love I believe

we shared was not

real, trickster, cheater

with your thoughts on her

dirty now, on stairs, I sit

something crawls inward

festering painfully

thoughts breed, disdainfully

No Longer Two

our souls will hibernate

movement ceases of the

faceless sun and absent moon

comet pulls an emblazed sign

cousins gone a fishing

drums pulse rain dance

willows wash sunbeams

dark clouds migratory

adolescent heart sprouts

weary stickers, aching

dissolving slowly

like sandspurs in flesh

at seventeen glorious he was

earthly salvation, my safe place

but now I hang cocooning

wrapping me in silk

the spider always gets his prey

not lovable, my tombstone will say

Sorrow's Flower

the strong sharp edges

of your body, slices bits

off my soft pink underbelly

garnets plunge hastily

inner recesses staining

sheets that I dry, a gift

softer than mulberry silk

gusts of spring winds whistle

tales of whispering woes

blue jays and wrens weep

dry eyes scratch when blinking

like an old dishcloth

on this aging but fragile face

sorrows, know their bloom

before budding like I know

soon I will be made to bend too far

my heart will drown and I will go

Waiting

Soaring with anointed fingertips, I touch
the cerulean starlit sky, weeping. Time, a
distant cousin of the moon, sighs. Words
thrown maliciously, where hurt is so often
like birdseed flung into the air without
contemplation.

Raw is my body, why must you toss me
like a thing whose mere determination is
survival of love? Guarding rusty cans
filling with blood from libretti out of
place, dangling as they beg for mercy.
Banging drums as your words ascend
with illuminating notes about painful
devotion. Skin stretches across the
concealment of my face from where the
tears flow.

Agony is a reminder of our existence, not
unlike the cavity that cannot be filled, so
it lays in wait, until it dawns a purpose.

Memories Buried In A Box

I am the seasoning in your food
infused with blood-tinged love
grave diggers plow a hole
into my left eye, now crossed
black memories are buried there,
along with my vision
lifeless in a woeful cardboard box,
are my wedding rings
my father's voice haunting me,
calling me a whore, and other things
why do we run to get away,
from abuse only to unearth more
deep joyless paths, maps of unborn words
burn into youthful cheeks with tears
seeds of love I was planting
hot stones echo Kentucky sounds
laying on trees, picking ferns
swimming in her smelly river
events before your deception cut
my flesh into an absent sliver
somewhere a child weeps and seeks
answers from God on their knees
a robin feeds her fledglings
until they are strong enough to live
my roots are old now and cover the earth

with oxygen, joy, and love

my child and her children

are now branches from my tree

those who love me listen with their spirit

for my home is by the sea

and my ancient soul is finally free

Part Three

Blooming

Incomplete, my soul floats in a bubble, a friend of the birds who traverses mountain tops in nuptial plumage. As they venture near, decreeing their tenderness, perceiving their feelings of love, they see a lone child, not a grown woman. Slivers of moments stretching into years of my young heart append my bubble with strings of Lotus silk.

Multifarious tastes of bitter life fashion a core of injurious smells and tastes that could besmirch fair hearts and lives. I cling to survival and to never produce a history following the steps of the imposters, monsters, or drunken parents, waging war to fight the birth of another generation of pain.

Epochs of anger maim this young woman as horns of ivory fracture this head which sees memoirs in sepia. Once love was tasted, like sweet, freshly harvested ears of buttery corn, I attested to never assenting to mere contentment. Fire wedged in my breast, and the sensation of only thirsting for my love was born. I was seventeen, and he was the light that sealed the dark dots from my eyes. Placing Dahlias and Honeysuckle, which cultivate on my body, spreading God's blessings while safely seeding his deep love within my heart.

Left for another, tears dine upon other tears and flesh slowly dissolves areas that your warm body had explored, leaving me in a continual state of thawing. My heart hung upon an oak and the catfish hollered from below the ponds, spreading words of mercy throughout the world of God's creatures. Yet, for a while, I slowly died upon that tree.

Lulling for years, I talked only to God and the trees. Education interrupted the black dots and the suffocating miasma ensconcing my horrific fear of life with two alcoholic parents. Then a babe was born, she floated sealed within my belly. Oh, how I saw this seed! Singing, dancing, and rejoicing, I treasured this delicate branch to which I was joined.

Legacies come with God's Holy Grace. A wise old soul at twenty-two, I spent six glorious months getting to know this child, while she swam without her floaties on her arms. She took my nourishment and grew into a gift of breezes floating gently with the smells of magnolia, gardenia, and jasmine. Like seasons in a rushing hourglass she grew and flourished. Beautiful were her ways of watching out for those who spent a whiff of sadness or pain.

What have I learned: Mirrors emulate the casing in which our soul floats. Those who have touched my heart with kindness live within me, nourishing my heart. I will visit here on this earth a little while. The beauty we find propels with the uncertainty of the squall, lying within that ever-changing soul. When I leave, I will do so as a bloom that is ready to molt the splendor held within. I will see the brilliance of the Face of God and I will finally be Home.

When I succumb, dear husband, please do not shed a tear for me! I will be that child I never got to be, dancing, and rejoicing without even the knowledge of sadness. I came from a seed, I grew as a seedling and God shined on my bloom and His Breath took me Home.

Sundry Cages

seeking refuge, sorrows spill
like drops of vinegar
in respite, I lay them down
on hairy green leaves, gesturing
upon a trellis of jasmine white
buds' scent like heaven's gate
a lion sleeps still this night
gorillas' rough hands touch sadness
grooming air as I breathe
trees know my heart
prayers go up for me
the sins of the father
the sins of the mother
does my core rest redolent
of childhood innocence,
freedom from sundry cages
sorrow, regret, and grasping
all are guilty, so we raise
sluicing our own body's sin
florets spring from fingertips
melodiously I lay me down
hands of the earth kiss me
peace beckons
hope is a songbird's sound

Growth

prayers answered like the great eagle

soaring first from a small rock

then a great boulder

rising from earth

my path

unsure

you cannot break me, shame me,

or even drive me to despair

I have faced my life

my story woven

from bone

and blood

memory sealed within an envelope

hiding in an invisible pocket

rejoicing, I feel love

my heart blooms

in all directions

safety settles

strong wind covers the ground

walking I spread seeds

where my feet have

danced among

the greatest

of trees

lessons of love and great joy

sadness and blessings

have cut into both

hands and feet

they linger

there

tear ducts long since dry

life a gift of my reason

making tender peace

with myself at last

white doves

sing

Open Casket

smells you loved during life
you now have in abundance
wildflowers grow in meadows
in the vase, they don't stand up
at attention, they lay playfully
gardenias your favorites, dance
close to your stiff, doll-like head
you would have been pleased
church seats were in demand
seeing people from the red brick house
my dress was bright, and its smells
were vanilla, jasmine, and lavender
the curve in your mouth was painted
red, and your hair was perfect, just dyed
why did you do it mom, sober for the
first time in two whole years now
since daddy took his life, so well planned
Saturday's coffee over the phone a treat
you talked of the smells on the pier
the flounder you would cook for friends
in the AA program that you gladly attend
why did you do it, mom, you sounded so grateful
you should have moved away, should've,

would've, could've, they say you get happy

once you make up your mind and there is a plan

singing swing low, sweet chariot, a cappella

the best I ever sang, not a dry eye in the church

two valiums did the trick, it seemed, I was great

problem was, I didn't feel anything mommy

come next Saturday, I made a great cup of fresh coffee

I dial your number, think of everything I needed to say

sorry, the number you dialed is no longer in service

dropping the phone, I collapsed on the floor

my heart can see your soul as it gracefully flies

meeting God in His fluffy home in the skies

we will hold each other, and I will love you

you will tell me you're sorry, and I will smile

I know, mommy, we found Grace, I am sorry too

Nature Brings Wedding Gifts

reflective night, the brink of life

brings youthful evenings to smiles

replete lovers sing and share a cup

of ashen moon a voyeur there

adoration, lay dreams of new home

for me it is you, for you it is me

stars show off their new red dresses

dew drapes the grass and trees

a bride vows her love near waves

charging white horses slowing

on wet sand nearing cabin door

once, a sad child, now adoring wife

energy seeps through tan skin

her husband kisses her again

hopeful heart gives all of herself

the sky grows red, the moon

places red silk slip, setting mood

crimson sunset lay on newlyweds

contentment shines on bodies nude

I Am

standing like a rock in a child story

incapable of puncturing with words or stones

for what can be done that hasn't already been done

resilient, balancing myself like

the great rocky mountain goats

ascending the craggy terrain

roam earth's surface unafraid

stages of my new liberating life

growing up a young and an old soul

in my later years I rejoice and enjoy

childhood with my best friend

food nourishing me as it never did before

laughter comes easy to my throat

like a welcomed guest that warms

the inside of me like a hot bowl of soup

filling me with love in all aspects of my life

torn and tattered no more, the child rests

Tribute to The Forest

Disentangling my body as my spirit flows without restraint through the dreams of the elusive creatures of the blessed forestland. My skin touches tiny petals of love that float freely, as cottonwood trees have turned the forest into a winter land.

As their fleecy white seeds blow into my dreamland with a subtle gust, reminiscent of the exquisite white feather of the Albino Cardinal. Long sought-after breezes turning sultry air cooler, and into melodies of the water lilies. Floating with caution scarcely touching the gentle Swan Neck moss, as I tiptoe to the sounds of the covered land beneath the forest.

Light brown is the speckled fur of a newborn fawn wrapped within itself, and helpless as it lay in a pine needle nest awaiting the solace of its mother.

Golden Dart male frogs calling out in their tempo to find a willful mate, its strength, a poison plentiful enough to slay ten unsullied humans.

Sing to me sanctioned memories of your charms for I cling so tender, bringing back your magic, blessed, with the forest of my youth. Swallow me in your belly, for God will bring me back to this splendor. Until then, my gentle friend, I will dream of you from above your sculpted tops. I will meet you there, where eagles fly, and children play and share their treasured honey drops.

Low Hanging Cloud

wren tap-dancing

on tepid rooftop

caterpillars visible

languid prisoners

in thick cocoon

like a low hanging cloud

on a timeworn oak

insects bathe in

raindrops left from

morning showers

inhaling nature's gift

fragrance of petrichor

mantis prays the scent

will persist for evermore

Bedtime

you whisper soft your stories
to my closed sated eyelids
your cold feet find mine
warming them, laughing
like children rub marbles
time stops noise like snow
insects and animals' slumber
darkness speckled with stars
I lie in comfort, undaunted
my world is no longer in dots
you are my earthly light
no monsters amble about
we say our prayers to God
fear is gone, like the last train
my parents rest, now out of pain
forgiveness blooms with new refrain

Love Me Like a Luna

petals drop from hazel eyes
moonbeams dust, cleaning skies
sleepy mushrooms deny they snore
vester bats taste an array of insects, then soar

honeysuckle nectar, kiss sweet
archaic willow oaks veil my treat
two hearts beat, amending our weather
heating up, whiffs of lavender and leather

his vest opens, wildflowers skip
naked, I bite my trembling red lip
luna moths mating, a vast debt to pay
death, for one evening in which, as two, we lay

your wings scatter in a breeze
leaving sticky eggs under leaves
dying my task achieved, yet no fear
together, my green lover, same time next year

Breakfast Is You

Fear no longer inches
into a miniscule crack
like a breeze to a window
carrying regret to sneer
ladybugs sit on ledge
playing bongos with dots
smells of coffee brewing
notes flying off your heart
dancing, my body moves
bonding, kisses float up
breathing I inhale love
scents teasing my flesh
red-headed woodpecker
plays his instrument in time
dancing our way as one
our morning breakfast, sublime

Wetlands

dance my darling

soulful moon designs

shadow movie on wetlands

fold into my craving arms

melt your craving

body, into elderly roots

souls unite in nostalgic rhythm

caress cypress tubers

stretching toward crimson

sky, seeking air for winded breath

float into me love

drink me now

one life, one heart

Green Eyes

waves of elusive aroma heighten

willowy hips, accenting tiny waist

cracks in floor seal for small feet

red silk cleaves to singing curves

as jasmine vines to ancient trellis

loose red locks sway to jazz notes

green eyes tell me my entrance

made ready your mood for love

your embrace, I am aching now

plentiful our fruit, a weighty bough

End of The Season

maple leaves folding

hiding their beauty

time running a race

with our highland past

unveiling to me

our crimson dreamlife

would never last

my ears blooming

clematis like trumpets

hearing only purrs of delight

unfurling my wings of white

sailing on jasmine clouds

waning into the night

Full of Treasures

treasures climb into my basket
sun whispers, I capture with dew
two wrens with a picnic for two

a lone red berry from a holly tree
anoles who are looking for heat
pearls, riches found deep in the sea

your heat in any winter's night
hiccups from a small toy poodle
my words, I am sorry, after a fight

claps, I hold in a bottle from an oak
giggles, from a baby finding his voice
books, bubbles for a warm tub soak

"Our Father," the words that I pray
written on mulberry silk leaves
your sweet kiss at the end of each day

Nature's Opera

weeping chestnut tree
lays her guarded head
upon tiers of yielding moss
mockingbirds orchestrate
legendary operatic play
in which timeworn cicadas
contract fierce belly muscles
deer cavort with newborn fawn
black-capped chickadees catch
tiny yellow moths stuck
upon the sticky spider's web
sun tips her hat at the squirrels
chasing one another's tails
while feasting on serene bluebells

Melding Into You

your generous lips a pathway

to warmth, in which I submerge

sweet our exchange like a cinnamon roll

dripping in soft yellow butter

deriving sensations, as I enter

your mouth drowning in you

lost again in our movements

we are dripping like the candle by the bed

blue notes tiptoe on your torso, I am like liquid

folding into your every crease

where are you, and where am I

for we are unaware as our smells unite

climbing inside you, we are one

as our heartbeat is a blue velvet petal

which floats into moments that are giving birth

to that which has no name

my morning, evening, and in between

may your love for me never cease

my beautiful, green-eyed husband

without you, I could never breathe

The Colors of Love

pink am I, fresh and innocent with you
opening like a virgin bud, giving birth to beauty
you are the intoxicating fragrance that pours over me
every time you breathe, a peach is slowly eaten
gardenias and jasmine jumping in midair like babes
on trampolines where nothing can stop us from flying
sweet music pours from your mouth into mine, and we
float in a yellow silk quilt made with the stories of our love
I feel my heart beating as I dive into cerulean water
your red light surges inside the intensity of our oneness
feet mingle under covers, and consciousness dips away
into the place where lovers long to go, as one spoon
we give thanks to God for one another and the years
that pass away as we pray one another don't go too soon

Mature Love

feet dance, intermingle

touches sing purring

skin melts as bark

molts from crepe myrtles

earth sable and cold

denied craving more

lust like a flower

needs her stem

using nature's manners

we seal eyes to old life

one heart we now share

never looking back twice

Us

whisper softly in my tender ear

as shadows of memories linger near

fire crackles breeds tender love forever soft

heat rising, warms up swiftly, our bedroom loft

laughter sparks seedlings of love with ageless years

sometimes sorrow invades dialog with liberating tears

we stay for love, not a paper commitment as we grow old

finding great comforts in God's blessings as our lives unfold

Dips of Life

flow of water
as rain dances
upon the tin roof
down the gutter
into water barrel
my newly planted
purple pansies
tiny stream draws
my heart, I ruminate
on daughter's tears
her prom date cancels
last minute, he is older
pain floods tender heart
how can I protect her
knowing that I can't
sorrow will visit again
holding her in my arms
wiping her salty tears
I tell her, you don't treat
a lady like that, let him go
she finds another
one of many challenges
in the life of a daughter

tiny dips that will make

her a strong woman

someday, the pansies

come back too

just like she does

when she's feeling blue

Kindness

unique her short scar
eyelashes flutter as
slow shutter speed
clicks small hole
slender cheek quivers
temperate is the wind
quick steps to the bend
feet travel with purpose
track movements noiseless
hearing steps on hollow
stones, I smell lavender
is that for me, I wonder
hearing wonderous thunder
frail like a wounded sparrow
wet hair whips around
sticking crosswise on face
opening my red umbrella
here take mine, I must insist
thank you, friend, it seems
kindness does indeed exist

Untethered

it was evening
gently I cast my line
a hapless being
catching the moon
resting beside me
her sadness flooding
brightness bleeding
lovers gaze upon me
make love in my shadow
lonesome, I too, need love
angels joining us
at my bequest
made me into a star
unhooking my line
we took to the sky
always together
now you and I

You Were the Best of Us

Daylilies and lavender fall from a sky of bright eyes,
in the silhouette of a boat under a quarter moon.
Born in the month of the ram
with your right fist on your pink cheek.
I was twenty, and you were my gift from God, my second
love.
My milk came like a white river on the third day.
Red, your color, dwelling within the passion
where fire seared black, my white peasant dress.
Burning away the smell of gardenias and honeysuckle,
a miracle fashioned within our fervidness.
Meeting your father in an arid desert on foreign sand,
oh, how I was craving dreams, escape, and freedom.
He was to be my savior, but he was only a man.
Like the red coral of the sea, our child, was the best of him
and me.

Sunflower – A New Page

I am a sunflower, golden, proud, and tall
dancing playfully toward the bright sun
no longer living in the land of the small

dots of death at night, bees that can sting
mom sewing me shut to curtain my truth
no longer huddling up a cowardly thing

hiding my food in panties so I could flee
seeking wisdom as stem and flower grow
consoling the wee child who once was me

doorways to who I am, my heart and soul
is my gift to give to those I choose to love
a survivor, my stem, leaf, and flower whole

for God so loved me, his innocent daughter
forgiveness I found, as I flourish with age
my ray florets feel His rain and curing water
life moving splendidly with every new page

Now I Am

the silent space breathing as the peregrine falcon flies
pollen dancing as I unfurl spreading my wisdom in seed
rocking to the rhythm of my beating heart's joyful song

God didn't take me then, for I am exactly where I belong

About the Artist

Francisco Bravo Cabrera
Also Known as Bodo Vespaciano

Francisco, artist/poet, is a graduate of Miami's Florida International University. He has been engaged in the art world since 1998 developing his "JaZzArt" and his "Surreal-Expressionism." He has exhibited in cities such as New York, Miami, Istanbul, Barcelona, Zaragoza, and Valencia. His compositions are made up of musical instruments and bodies that exist in his worlds of jazz and fantasy. His endeavour is to create paintings that communicate and transmit a message of hope, peace, and togetherness. Francisco has donated the illustrations and the cover art for this book knowing full well that art and poetry are two forms of the same creative urge that comes from the soul and enrich our spirit.

"One must be true to oneself. I am a painter of my day, giving in that manner, spirituality to my work. Talent is the result of hard work, but art is a gift from God and to God goes the glory."

Francisco Bravo Cabrera, paintinginvalencia.com.

NOTA BENE

"I love the written word, and poetry is the perfect medium for truly expressing the values, emotions, and feelings that we share. I greatly admire and believe in Joni as a writer. She is a wonderful writer who touches the heart, so I have donated these drawings that you see here as illustrations to her love-filled, powerful, and deeply personal poetry."
(Francisco Bravo Cabrera, Valencia, Spain,
paintinginvalencia.com)

About the Author

Joni Karen Caggiano is an internationally published author, poet, and photographer. She was a 2022 Pushcart Nominee for her poem, "Old News is Not Old News," published by The Short of It Publishing. She was privileged to write the Foreword for the Best Seller, *I Am In Itself Poetry In The Dark,* by the five-time Amazon Best Selling Author Michelle Ayon Navajas. On *SpillWords Press NYC,* Joni won Publication of the Month in November 2022 and Co-Winner of Socialite of the Year 2023 and 2024. Joni was a Co-Author of both #1 Amazon Bestselling books, *Hidden In Childhood* and *Wounds I Healed.* She is also in seven additional Poetry Anthologies. Her first book of poetry, Joni is also proud to be included in the poetry anthology, *A Safe and Brave Space,* published by Garden of Neuro Publishing (2024). She is currently a writer for *Hotel Masticadores.* Joni formerly contributed four combined pieces a month for one year to *MasticadoresIndia* and *MasticadoresUSA*. Joni is a retired nurse, ACOA (Adult Children of Alcoholics) survivor, and environmental advocate.

the-inner-child.com
Twitter: @theinnerchild1
Instagram: @jonicaggiano
Author's Blog

www.ingramcontent.com/pod-product-compliance
Lightning Source LLC
Chambersburg PA
CBHW021647120626
46545CB00002B/746